The Science of...

ELECTRICITY

Julia Vogel and Jared Siemens

openlightbox.com

LIGHTBOX

Go to **www.openlightbox.com** and enter this book's unique code.

ACCESS CODE

LBD77875

Lightbox is an all-inclusive digital solution for the teaching and learning of curriculum topics in an original, groundbreaking way. Lightbox is based on National Curriculum Standards.

OPTIMIZED FOR

- ✓ **TABLETS**
- ✓ **WHITEBOARDS**
- ✓ **COMPUTERS**
- ✓ **AND MUCH MORE!**

STANDARD FEATURES OF LIGHTBOX

AUDIO High-quality narration using text-to-speech system

VIDEOS Embedded high-definition video clips

ACTIVITIES Printable PDFs that can be emailed and graded

WEBLINKS Curated links to external, child-safe resources

SLIDESHOWS Pictorial overviews of key concepts

INTERACTIVE MAPS Interactive maps and aerial satellite imagery

QUIZZES Ten multiple choice questions that are automatically graded and emailed for teacher assessment

KEY WORDS Matching key concepts to their definitions

VIDEOS

WEBLINKS

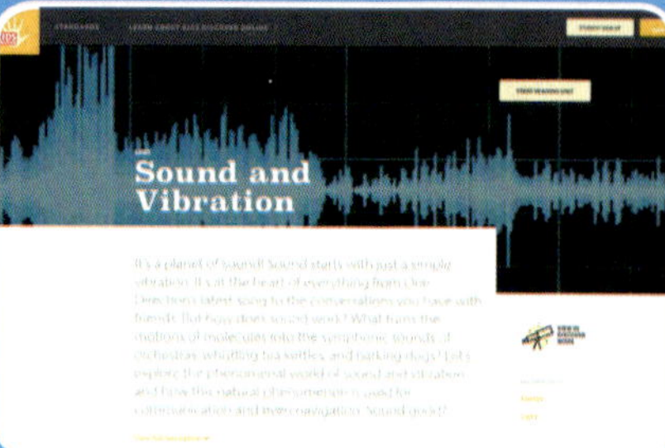

SLIDESHOWS

QUIZZES

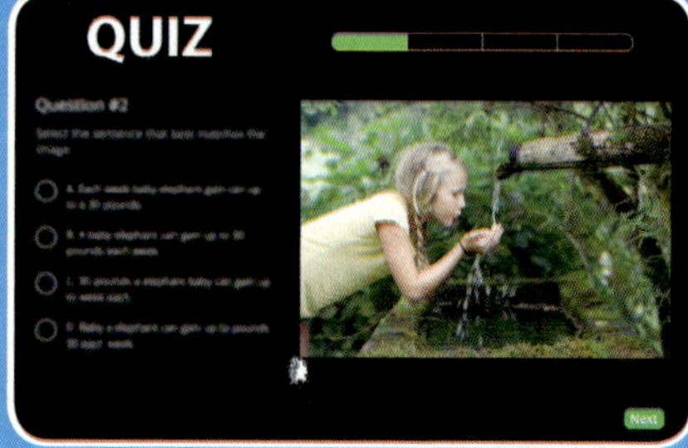

The Science of...

ELECTRICITY

CONTENTS

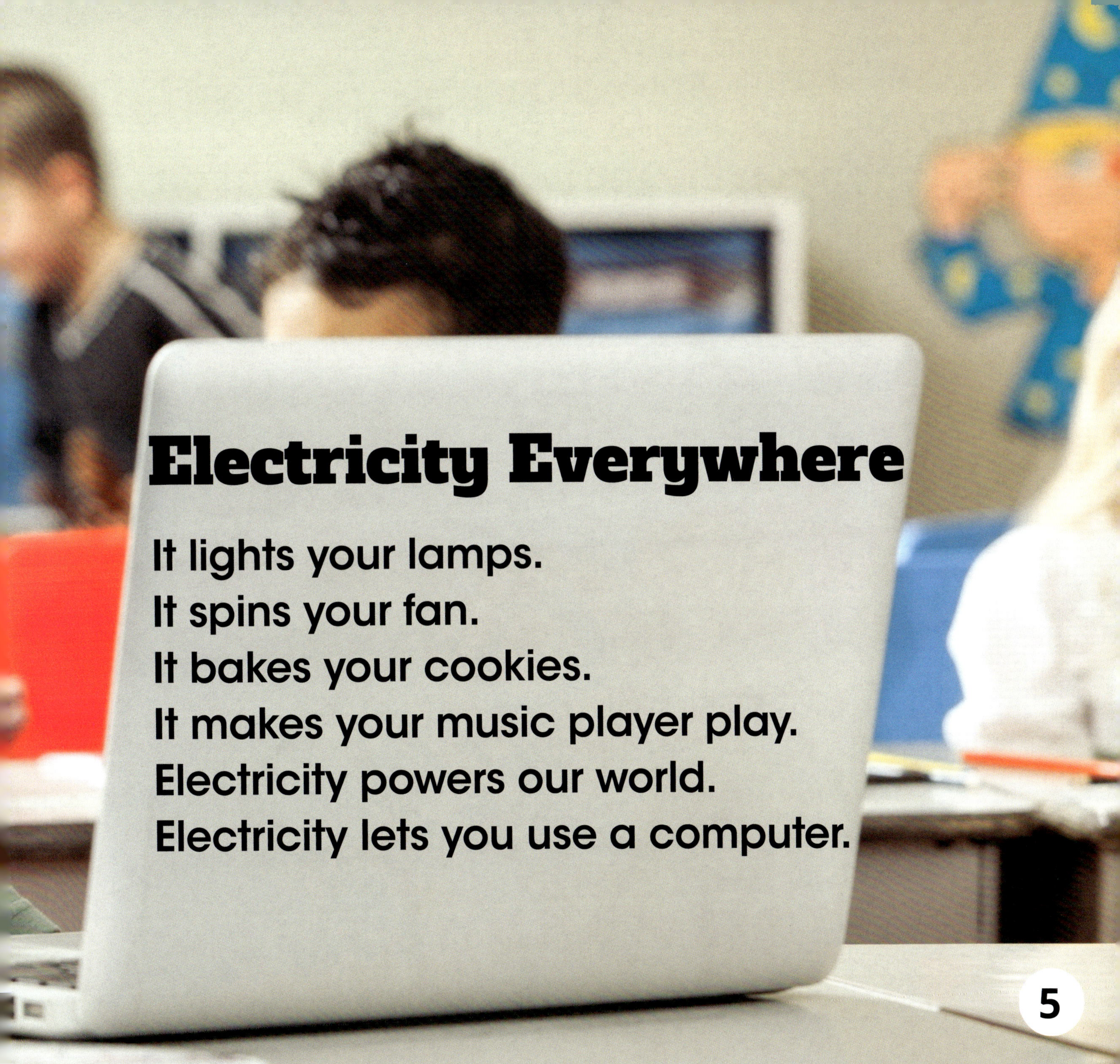

Electricity Everywhere

It lights your lamps.
It spins your fan.
It bakes your cookies.
It makes your music player play.
Electricity powers our world.
Electricity lets you use a computer.

Electricity is part of everything. It is electrons on the move. What are electrons? They are bits of tiny atoms. Atoms make up every object—rocks, clouds, trees, and you!

Hair, skin, bones—they're all made of atoms. You need a super strong microscope to see atoms.

Charge!

Shuffle your feet across the carpet. Then touch a doorknob. Zap! Electrons from the carpet moved to your body. Then they jumped from your finger to the metal knob. Zing! That shock was static electricity.

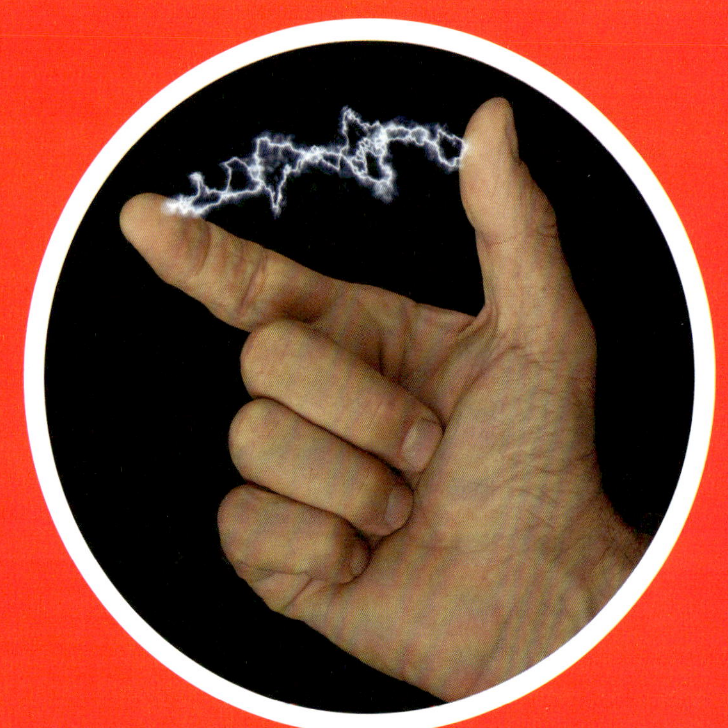

Static electricity is making this girl's hair stick out.

Static electricity in lightning is incredibly powerful.

Lightning is static electricity, too.
Electrons build up in a storm cloud.
They jump from cloud to cloud or
down to the ground.
Flash! Lightning streaks through the sky.

The power in lightning can split a tree. The heat can burn down a house. It can start a forest fire. Lightning cracked this tree in half.

Lightning's shock can be deadly. When you see lightning, stay inside! If you see lightning, get indoors right away.

Go with the Flow

Scientists discovered how to make electricity another way. Scientists put magnets inside coils of wire. This small motor uses magnets and wires to make electricity.

Then they moved the magnets back and forth. This excited electrons in the wires. The electrons flowed like a river. Their flow made an electric current.

Power plants have huge machines with magnets and wires. A power source keeps the magnets spinning. The machines make a powerful electric current.

Grand Coulee Dam in Washington makes more power than any other dam in the United States.

Water is the power source at this plant. Electricity flows into long wires carried on tall towers.

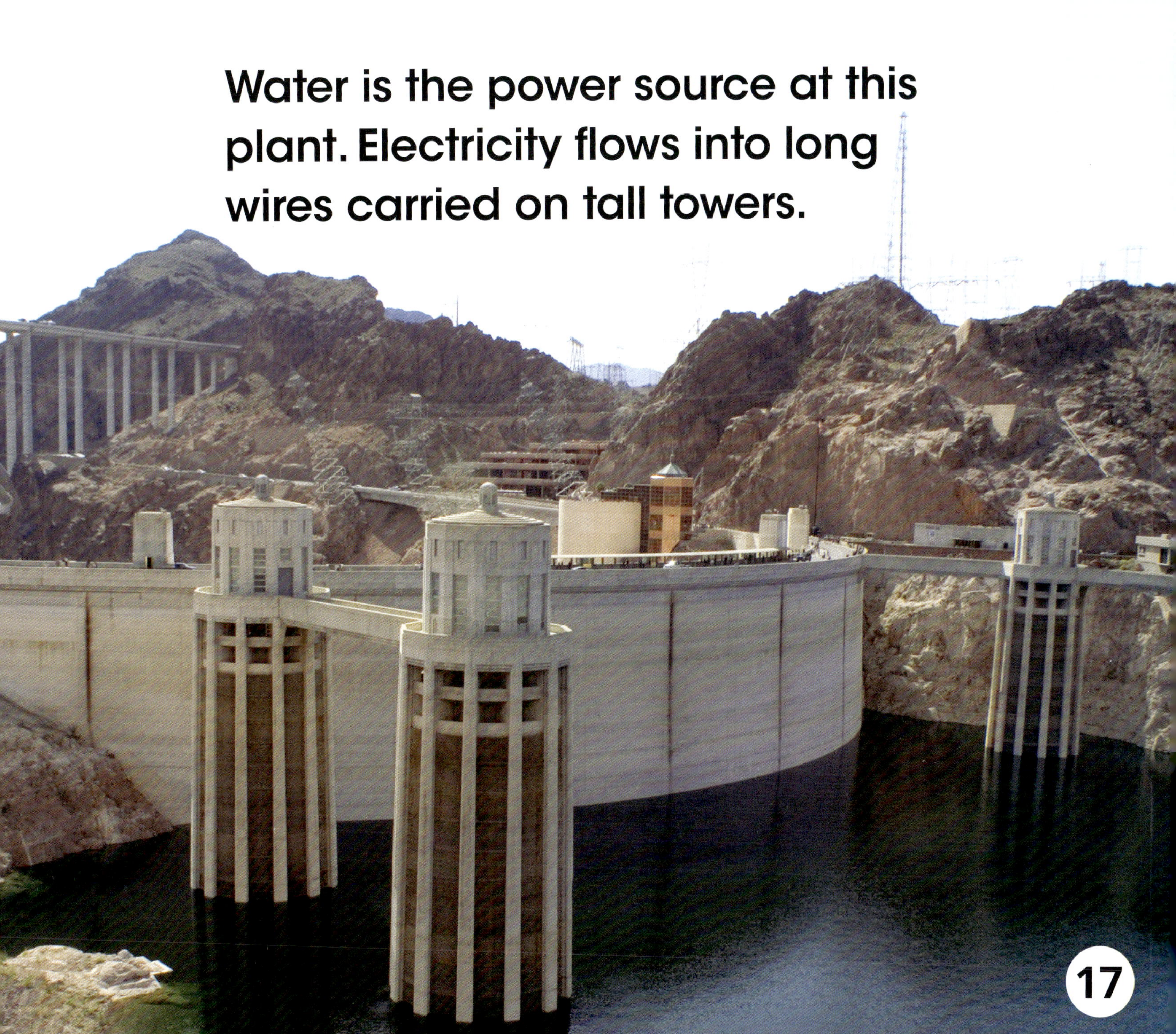

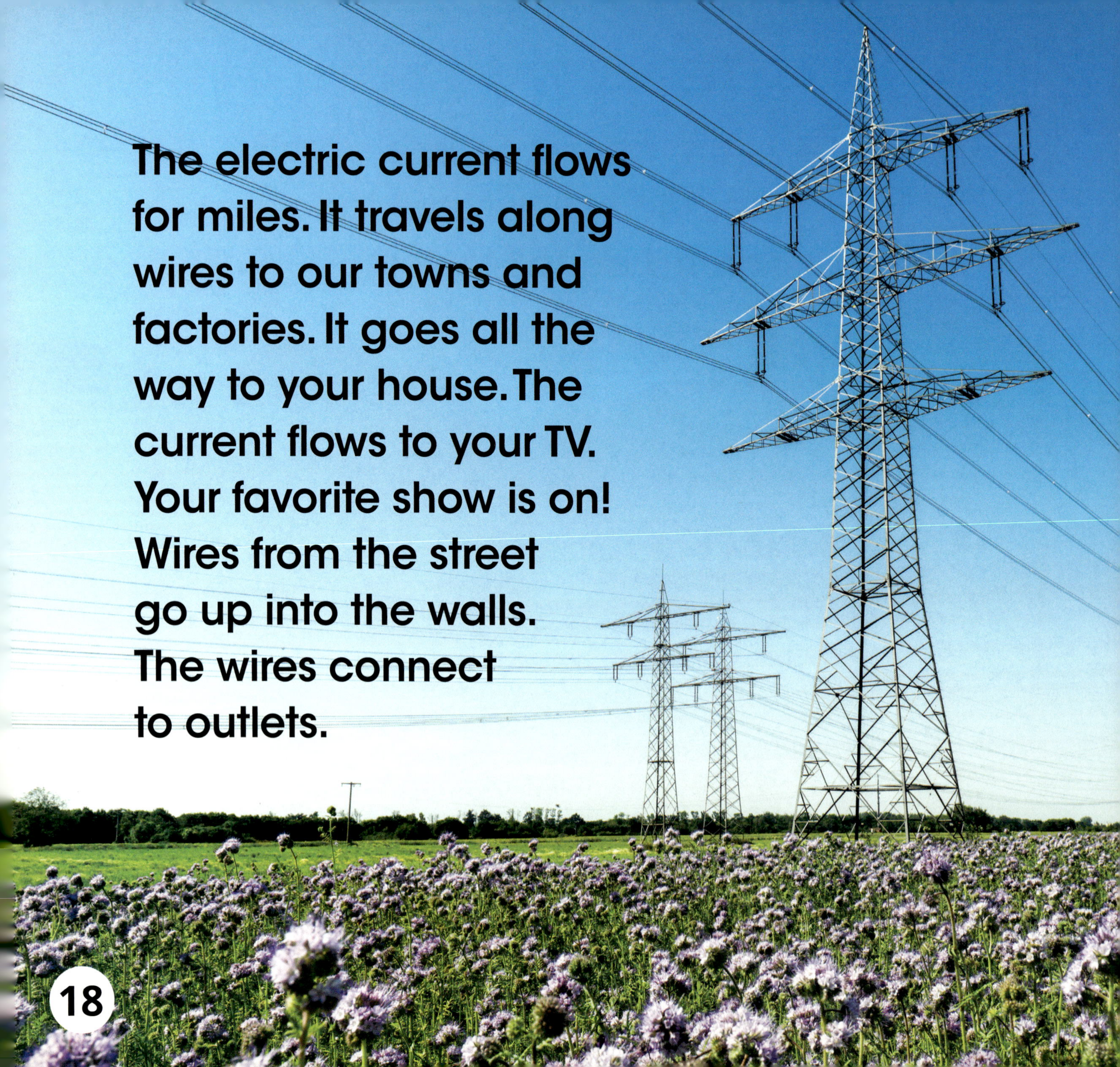

The electric current flows for miles. It travels along wires to our towns and factories. It goes all the way to your house. The current flows to your TV. Your favorite show is on! Wires from the street go up into the walls. The wires connect to outlets.

You can turn off the TV with one push of a button. An electric current must flow in a loop, or circuit. The button can stop the flow. Push it again and close up the circuit. Your show is back on. Electricity comes from the battery. It flows to the buttons and back again.

Unplug and Have Fun!

Imagine our world without electricity. It's a blackout! We all use electricity. It's important not to waste it. Saving electricity is a bright idea! Electricity isn't free. So saving electricity saves your family money. Also, many power plants use coal to fuel their machines. That pollutes the air. Saving electricity can help Earth, too. What are some fun ways to cut back on electricity?

Electricity Facts

Lightning **strikes** places all over Earth about **100 times** each second.

It takes about **half a pound** (0.25 kilograms) of coal to power a **TV** for **4** hours.

More than **75 million** homes in the United States get their electricity from **water power**.

The United States uses **more electricity** for **Christmas lights** than some countries use in a **whole year**.

Turning off a computer at night can save about **$40 a year** in electricity bills.

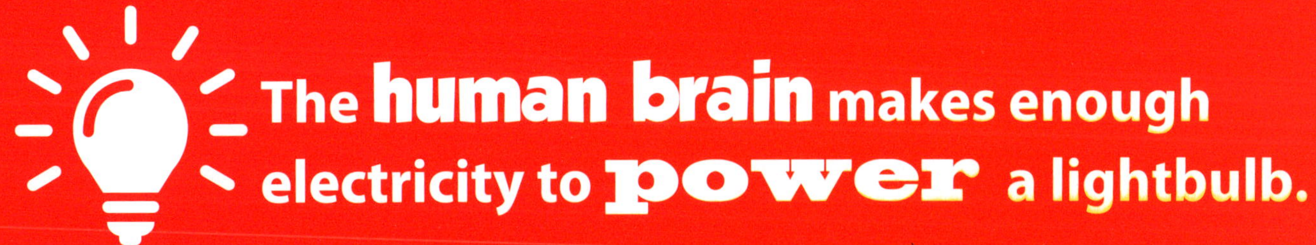

The **human brain** makes enough electricity to **power** a lightbulb.

KEY WORDS

Research has shown that as much as 65 percent of all written material published in English is made up of 300 words. These 300 words cannot be taught using pictures or learned by sounding them out. They must be recognized by sight. This book contains 102 common sight words to help young readers improve their reading fluency and comprehension. This book also teaches young readers several important content words, such as proper nouns. These words are paired with pictures to aid in learning and improve understanding.

Page	Sight Words First Appearance
5	a, it, lets, lights, makes, our, play, use, world, you, your
6	and, are, every, is, move, of, on, part, the, they, trees, up, what
7	all, made, need, see, too
8	feet, from, that, then, was
9	girl, out, this
10	in
11	down, or, through, too
12	can, house, start
13	away, be, get, if, right, when
14	another, go, how, put, small, way, with
15	an, back, like, river, their
16	any, have, keeps, more, other, plants, states, than
17	at, into, long, water
18	along, for, miles, show
19	again, close, comes, must, off, one, stop, turn
21	air, also, cut, earth, family, help, idea, important, it's, many, not, so, some, we, without

Page	Content Words First Appearance
5	computer, cookies, electricity, fan, lamps, music player
6	atoms, clouds, electrons, object, rocks
7	bones, hair, microscope, skin
8	body, carpet, doorknob, finger, knob, shock, static electricity
10	lightning
11	ground, sky, storm cloud
12	forest fire, heat, power
13	indoors, inside
14	flow, magnets, motor, scientists, wire
15	electric current
16	dam, Grand Coulee Dam, machines, power source, United States, Washington
17	towers
18	factories, outlets, street, towns, TV, walls
19	battery, button, circuit, loop, push
21	blackout, coal, money

Published by Smartbook Media Inc.
350 5th Avenue, 59th Floor New York, NY 10118
Website: www.openlightbox.com

Library of Congress Control Number: 2017942924

ISBN 978-1-5105-2415-6 (hardcover)
ISBN 978-1-5105-2416-3 (multi-user eBook)

062017
022217

Printed in the United States of America in Brainerd, Minnesota
1 2 3 4 5 6 7 8 9 0 21 20 19 18 17

Project Coordinator: Jared Siemens
Designer: Ana María Vidal

Every reasonable effort has been made to trace ownership and to obtain permission to reprint copyright material. The publishers would be pleased to have any errors or omissions brought to their attention so that they may be corrected in subsequent printings.

The publisher acknowledges iStock, Alamy, and Getty Images as its primary image suppliers for this title.